Living in France

by Ani Hawkinson
and Patrick R. Moran

Fourth, Revised Edition

PRO LINGUA ⬛ ASSOCIATES

Published by Pro Lingua Associates
15 Elm Street
Brattleboro, Vermont 05301 USA
802-257-7779   800-366-4775
Email prolingu@sover.net

SAN 216-0579

Copyright © 1984, Revised 1992, 1994, 1998
by World Learning, formerly
The Experiment in International Living

ISBN 0-86647-111-1

This book was originally developed and published by The Experiment in International Living, Brattleboro, Vermont, as part of its Orientation Development Project. The initial development funds were provided by the U.S. Information Agency under the President's International Youth Exchange Initiative. Pro Lingua is grateful for permission to revise and publish this edition.

The staff of the original development project were: Ani Hawkinson, writer; Alvino Fantini, director and editor; Julie Soquet, project and orientation director. The second, third, and fourth editions were revised by Patrick R. Moran and edited by AA Burrows.

This fourth edition was revised with the help of Anne and Bruno Jost of Nantes, France. The first edition was reviewed for cultural accuracy by Claire Stanley of the U.S. Experiment and Nancy Mettlen and her colleagues at the French Experiment office. Peter deJong, former Secretary General, and the Directors of the various Experiment in International Living National Offices identified the original content areas covered in this country-specific series.

Illustrations by A. Mario Fantini and from Art Explosion 125,000 Images, © 1996 Nova Development Corporation; Corel Gallery © 1994 Corel Corporation; photographs by FotosEastlund, Wantagh, New York.

Designed and set by Judy Ashkenaz of Total Concept Associates in Brattleboro, Vermont, using Palatino text and Mistral display types. Cover design by AA Burrows. Printed by BookCrafters of Chelsea, Michigan.

Fourth, revised edition 1998
Printed in the United States of America

Contents

1. First Steps   1

1. Money   2
2. Food   3
   Courses of a traditional French meal   3
   Breakfast   4
   French wine   4
   French cheese   5
3. Restaurants   6
4. Hotels   7
5. Telephone   8
6. Transportation   9
   Airlines   9
   Trains   9
   Taxis   11
   Métro   11
   Buses   11
7. Letters, Telegrams, Faxes, and Email   12
8. Shopping   12
9. Health and Medical Care   14
10. Security   14
11. Tipping   14
12. Electricity   15
13. Conversions   16

2. Customs and Values   19

1. Greetings and Leave-takings   20
2. Names and Titles   21
3. Forms of Address   21
4. Conversation Topics and Styles   22
5. Invitations   23
6. Privacy   24
7. Personal Appearance   24
8. Time   24
9. Meals   25

iii

CONTENTS

10. Family 27
11. Daily Life 27
12. Leisure 28
13. Cafés 28
14. National Pride 29

3. Country Facts 30

1. History 30
2. Maps 40
3. Land and People 42
4. Government 44
5. Economy 45
6. Education 46
7. Religion 48
8. Art 49

4. The French Language 53

1. Some Basic Grammar 54
2. Useful French Phrases 66

5. Some Books about France 69

Perhaps the best known symbol of modern France, the Eiffel Tower, built for the World Exhibition of 1889 by engineer Gustav Eiffel to commemorate the centennial of the French Revolution, and summer tour boats reflected in the River Seine in Paris

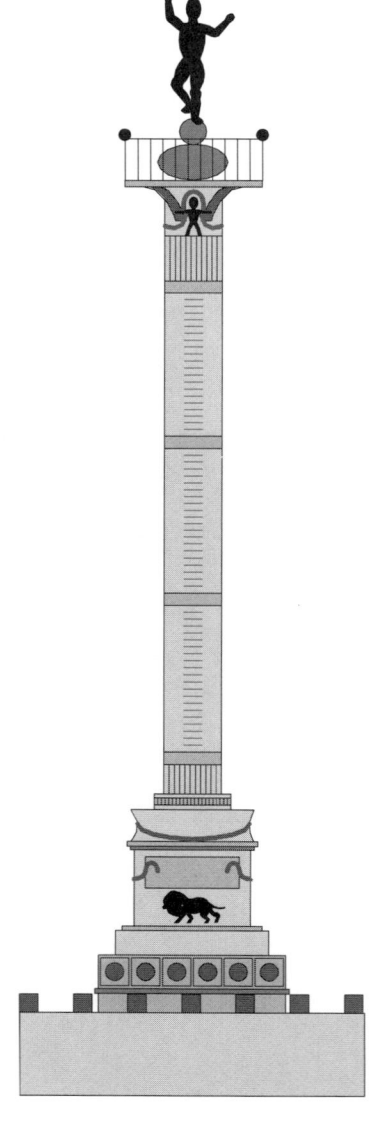

1. First Steps

Congratulations! You are about to embark upon an adventure—living in another country. Your destination is France. When you arrive, you will need to be able to satisfy some immediate survival needs. Often you will find that you must do things differently from how you do them at home. This section is designed to help you get started learning how to live in France. Although every town will be a little different, we can provide you with basic facts about life in France. Filling in the details will be up to you. So, for instance, while we can tell you about restaurants and eating habits in France, you will need to find places to eat which have food you like and can afford. And while we can tell you about various means of transportation existing in France, you will still need to find the best way to get around the particular town where you live. We can suggest alternatives, but you will be making the final choices.

One final note: You may find that cultural changes, technological advances, and regional differences affect customs, values, systems, and even the "country facts" as reported in this booklet. So "expect the unexpected" and be prepared to learn as well from your own direct experience. The information in this section and those which follow should be used only as an initial guide. ***Bonne chance!***

This section covers the topics listed below. Read the ones of most interest to you now; then read the others as the need arises.

1. Money
2. Food
3. Restaurants
4. Hotels
5. Telephone
6. Transportation
7. Letters and Telegrams
8. Shopping
9. Health and Medical Care
10. Security
11. Tipping
12. Electricity
13. Conversions

FIRST STEPS

1. Money

France is moving along with the rest of the European Economic Community towards adopting the Euro as its monetary unit. Until that happens, however, the *franc* is still used in France. Its value changes according to the world money market, so you must check the current exchange rate before you leave for France.

French *francs* are based on a decimal system, so that one *franc* contains 100 *centimes*. French money comes in the following denominations: 5, 10, and 20 *centime* coins; 1/2, 1, 2, 5, and 10 *franc* coins; and 20, 50, 100, and 500 *franc* banknotes.

It is culturally interesting that *le nouveau franc* ("the new franc," abbreviated F) has been used in France since 1960, but many older people still designate prices of things in terms of *anciens francs* when speaking. One *nouveau franc* equals 100 *anciens francs*. If you don't know about this tradition and are not able to recognize whether a price is being cited in old or new *francs*, you will find this confusing. In shops, cafés, and restaurants, written prices must always be in *nouveaux francs*. Although the term *nouveau(x)* is neither written nor spoken, it is understood.

Banks are open in France from 9:00 A.M. to noon and 2:00 to 4:00 or 5:00 P.M., Monday through Friday. Exchange offices are open in the *Gare de Lyon* and at the *Invalides* air terminal in Paris on Saturdays, Sundays, and in the evening. Usually there are offices for exchanging money at the larger train stations, airports, and air terminals. Hotels will also change money, but the exchange rate will not be as high as a bank will give you because the hotel charges a fee for providing the service. Similarly, while you can use travelers' checks when you make purchases in the large department stores, the rate will not be as good as at a bank. If you find yourself short of cash, a good rule of thumb is to exchange only small sums of money at shops, hotels, or restaurants, and to change larger sums at banks during their regular hours. Automatic teller machines are now widely available in French airports, train stations, hotels, shopping centers, and banks. These are a very convenient and safe way of getting cash. Contact your U.S. bank before leaving home to find out which ATM systems you can use in France and what limits and charges may apply. Your ATM and credit cards and your PINs may have to be reprogrammed for use in France. You can also ask about a Global Access debit card. Major credit cards are also widely accepted.

2. Food

France is well known for the variety and quality of its food, and you will have the opportunity to taste many things you may not have tried before. A typical French meal consists of several dishes served one after another, rather than all at the same time. First there is an *hors d'oeuvre,* then sometimes an *entrée,* followed by a meat and a vegetable, which may be served separately. The meal is usually completed with salad, cheese, dessert, and coffee.

Courses of a traditional French meal

Hors d'oeuvres vary from an assortment of raw vegetables, to fruits such as melons and tomatoes, to fish such as sardines in oil, smoked salmon, or shellfish. It is usual to have an *hors d'oeuvre* at the noon meal and a soup at the evening meal.

Entrées also vary, and it is here that you may taste new foods—frogs' legs, pigs' feet, snails, and tripe, to name but a few. Freshwater and marine fish of all types are also served, as are egg dishes such as omelettes. This course is sometimes omitted, since the meal is sufficient without it.

Meat may be served broiled, grilled, roasted, or in a sauce. Beef, lamb, pork, and poultry are all common, as are certain game animals. Some meats that may be new for you are goose, guinea-fowl, pigeon, pheasant, rabbit, veal, and horse meat.

Common vegetables are potatoes, green or white (dry) beans, peas, spinach, cauliflower, zucchini, and eggplant. Noodles may be served instead of potatoes.

FIRST STEPS

Bread is an integral part of all meals in France. It is eaten with almost all parts of the meal, except dessert. A meal without bread is inconceivable for most French people.

France is famous for both its wines and its cheeses, and different regions have their own specialties. Try to sample what is made in the region where you live.

To end the meal, the French will sometimes have dessert and coffee. Typical desserts include fruit, ice cream, pastries, and certain special dishes such as sweet *soufflés* and chocolate *mousse*.

Breakfast

The French generally eat a light breakfast, a "continental breakfast." This generally consists of coffee and bread and rolls (often *croissants*) served with butter and jam or marmalaide. You may ask for juice or fruit, milk, tea, or cocoa. Other breakfast foods such as eggs and cereals are generally available in restaurants and cafés.

French coffee is generally rich and strong. It is commonly served with hot milk, particularly at breakfast, when in homes it is often served in a bowl. In restaurants, you can ask for American coffee and decaf.

French wine

Some regions of France are especially famous for the wines they produce, but there are vineyards all over the country. Probably the most famous areas for table wine are Burgundy (*Bourgogne*) and *Bordeaux*. *Champagne* is known everywhere for its bubbly wine enjoyed on festive occasions, as *Cognac* is for its fine brandies. Other regions known for their wines are *Beaujolais*, the Southwest region near *Bordeaux*, the *Loire* and *Rhône* Valleys, *Provence, Alsace, Languedoc-Roussillon,* and the island of Corsica. In many regions both red and white wines are produced; they range from elegantly dry to robust and sweet. French wines are always judged by their smell (*bouquet*), color, and the interest and complexity of their taste.

The character of the wine comes from the way it is grown and processed, but also from the land, the climate, and the type of grape used. There are many varieties of grape. For white wine, these include *Chardonnay*, *Chenin Blanc*, and *Sauvignon Blanc*. Among the many grapes used in red wine are *Cabernet Sauvignon*, *Merlot*, and *Pinot Noir*. The quality of wine is classified as follows: The finest and most expensive is *Appellation d'Origine Controlée* (AOC). Below that is *Appellation d'Origine Vins de Qualité Supérieure* (AOVDQS). More common but often delicious are the *Vins de Pays* (country wines) and the less expensive *Vins de Table* (table wines).

French cheese

There are more than 100 types of cheese (*fromage*) in France, and over 300 different varieties of them. Some, like *Roquefort* (a blue cheese), and *brie* and *camembert* (soft-ripened cheeses) are known the world over. The French also enjoy fresh cheeses, goat's milk cheeses (*chévre*), and semi-firm mountain cheeses like *Emmental*. Cheese is almost always enjoyed with red wine and bread. It is best served at room temperature.

FIRST STEPS

3. Restaurants

While meals in French restaurants are often expensive, they are usually quite delicious. You have the choice of ordering a set menu—usually consisting of two or three courses followed by cheese, dessert, and coffee—or ordering *à la carte*. It is usually a better buy to order the set menu, called *prix fixe*, and these are almost always posted outside the restaurant with their prices so you can see what you will be spending before you go in. Ordering the set menu is also a good way to get acquainted with French dishes you might not otherwise have thought to try.

A few things you might want to know about French restaurants are described here. First, you will be considered odd if you order just one dish. If you do so for reasons of economy, you may find that you are being charged the same price for a main dish alone as you would be for an appetizer plus a main dish. This, of course, is not true in smaller eating places such as cafés and snack bars. Also, it is not acceptable to have soft drinks with a meal in a restaurant, although it is all right in cafés and snack bars.

The best food is not necessarily found in the fanciest-looking restaurants. The French are more interested in what happens in the kitchen than in how comfortable the dining area is. The least expensive places to eat are *bistros* and cafés, which are often family-run. *Brasseries* are café-restaurants that are often large and noisy, with good, simple cooking.

Bread comes with the meal, but it is not served with butter. Water is not automatically served in French restaurants. You may ask for it, but be prepared for the fact that is is not usually served with ice. It is easiest to order bottled water, and both carbonated (*eau gazeuse*) and noncarbonated varieties are available. If you want plain tap water, you will need to ask for it by saying *l'eau plate, l'eau de robinet,* or *une carafe d'eau.*

Tips for service are almost always included in the bill for your meal or snack in France. If you like the service very much, however, you can leave an additional tip for the waiter.

To find out more about meal customs, read sections 9 and 13 in the chapter on "Customs and Values."

4. Hotels

Most hotels are required by French law to post the price of each room on its wall and to charge no more than the posted rate, which is set by the government. This does not apply to deluxe hotels, where prices are not subject to government control. The letters *TTC—toutes taxes comprises* ("all taxes included")—are used in many places. If you do not see them, you would be wise to ask what the additional charges are before you decide whether to stay at a particular hotel.

Breakfast is included in the price of the room at many French hotels. The breakfast is continental in style, consisting of black coffee or *café au lait,* hot chocolate, or tea with rolls, butter, and jam. If breakfast is not available at the hotel, you will always be able to get it in a nearby *bistro* or café.

In France, it is possible to stay in inexpensive *pensions* that cater to teachers and students. The price for some or all of your meals is included in the room cost; if you miss a meal it is your loss, not the *pension* owner's. In many *pensions* there is a minimum-stay period; you may not be able to stay for only a single night.

Three other possible types of accommodation can be investigated. Information about staying in small hotels and modest rural inns is available through the *Fédération Nationale des Logis et Auberges de France* ("dwellings and inns of France"), 25 rue Jean Mermoz, 75008 Paris. Information about bed-and-breakfast

FIRST STEPS

lodgings *(chambres d'hôte)* throughout rural France is available through the *Fédération Nationale des Gîtes Ruraux de France* ("humble rural dwellings of France"), 34 rue Godot de Mauroy, 75009 Paris. Many of these bed-and-breakfast accommodations are in the homes of families, so this source represents an opportunity to see France in a more personal way. Information about youth hostels is available through *Fédération Unie des Auberges de Jeunesse,* 10 rue Notre-Dame-de-Lorette, 75009 Paris.

5. Telephone

The telephone system in France is very modern and efficient. It is operated by the State as part of the postal system, *Poste, Télégraphe, Téléphone (PTT).* The modernization of the French telephone system was made a national priority in the 1970s, and the results are in place today. One such innovation is the *minitel,* a small computer attached to private telephones that allows subscribers to carry out all sorts of transactions from their homes, from reserving train tickets or reviewing entertainment schedules to corresponding by electronic mail.

Public telephones operate in two ways: by cards and by coins. The cards, *télécartes,* are similar to plastic credit cards, and you can buy them at railway stations, *magasins de presse,* and *tabacs.* The card contains 50 or 120 magnetically imprinted units; when you have used up these units through local or long distance telephone calls, you can renew your card. To make a call with this card, you insert it into the slot on the telephone, and dial your number. A small screen shows you how many units you have used for your call. Public telephones that require *télécartes* are very common; in large cities, it may be difficult to find a public telephone that operates on coins.

Coin-operated public phones use coin denominations of 1, 2, 5, and 10 francs, as well as 50 centimes. These telephones often require that you push a button to engage the call once the call has been answered. Be sure to read the instructions on the machine before you make the call.

Long distance and international calls can be very expensive when charged to hotel rooms in France. It is best to get an inter-

FIRST STEPS

national calling card and learn how to use it. Since hotels sometimes block the use of some cards, you may find it helpful to have more than one card, or you may want to place your calls from a pay phone.

6. Transportation

Airlines

Air travel both to and within France is generally convenient, though expensive. Air France is one of the world's great international airlines and has many good flights available to Paris and other French cities. Most other international airlines also fly into the two Paris airports, Orly Airport and Charles de Gaulle or Roissy Airport. Air travel is available within France via Air Inter, but it is more expensive and less popular than rail travel. Money-saving air travel passes are available, but they must be bought outside of France.

Trains

France has one of the world's most progressive railway systems. The *SNCF* (*Société Nationale des Chemins de Fer Français*) is owned and operated by the State. The entire system has been modernized, and the majority of lines use electric trains. It is possible to travel to any part of France from Paris without making it an overnight journey.

The fastest trains, called *TGV* (*Train à Grande Vitesse*), only go between certain cities. They can reach speeds of 378 km per hour (236 miles/hour). Seat reservations are required. If you travel

FIRST STEPS

on TGV trains during peak hours, you will have to pay a surcharge; otherwise, you pay the regular fare. Trains are distinguished according to whether they make no stops between departure point and destination (*les rapides*), stop only at large cities (*les express*), or stop at all towns (*les omnibus*). Almost all express trains also require a surcharge, which should be paid at the ticket counter before boarding the train.

SNCF has established special reductions if you travel at certain times during the day. Generally, the reductions are available if you travel any time except from 3:00 P.M. Friday to noon Saturday, and 3:00 P.M. Sunday to noon Monday, plus a few public holidays and certain summer holiday departure and return dates. Be sure to investigate the types of reductions available if you are planning to travel.

It is important to know that you must get your ticket (and surcharge card, if required) punched in the orange machines at the station before you depart. If you do not, you can be fined. There are signs on these machines telling you to do so: *Compostez votre billet*. To punch your ticket, put it in the machine where marked and move it slightly to the left until you hear a click.

To get a good seat, it is advisable to get to the station at least half an hour before the departure time. This is particularly important in big cities and at busy times.

If you plan to travel around France or in other parts of Europe, you may want to consider getting a rail pass. This is an economical way to travel by train for a specific period of time. There are several kinds of passes, some combined with air and car rental discounts. Among these are the France Rail, France Rail 'n Fly, France Rail 'n Drive, and France Fly, Rail, 'n Drive passes, as well as EuroPass, EurailPass, Eurail Youthpass, and Eurail Flexipass. Information on these passes is available from the French Government Tourist offices around the world (call 900-990-0040; 90¢/minute, from most guidebooks, or from your travel agent. You must buy these passes before you leave for France.

FIRST STEPS

Taxis

Taxis can be found in cities throughout France. Radio-equipped taxis are available and, if you call them, they will usually arrive to pick you up at precisely the time they promise. When hailing a taxi in town, don't be surprised if the driver of an empty cab gestures at you without stopping—the driver may simply be indicating that he or she is going home for a meal or has finished for the day. Taxi fares are not cheap. Of course, tipping the driver is appreciated, but it is not obligatory. Rates are usually posted inside the vehicle. It is important to be aware that rates increase about 20% from 10:00 P.M. to 6:30 A.M.

Métro

The *métro* in Paris is rapid and efficient. There are many lines covering every area of the city and connecting with one another at certain stations. Lines are identified by the names of the stations at their terminal points and a number. When changing from one line to another, all you need to do is follow the name of the terminal point of the line in the direction you are traveling. For instance, if you are changing onto the Vincennes-Neuilly line (the line connecting these two terminal points), and you are headed in the direction of Neuilly, follow the signs that say Neuilly, not the signs that say Vincennes.

Buses

Buses operate in all French cities as well as between cities and towns. Different routes are identified by number, and at each bus stop there are signs that show the numbers of the buses that stop there. In Paris, bus and *métro* tickets are interchangeable. Like *métro* tickets, bus tickets are sold individually or in 10-ticket *carnets*. Buses run from 6:30 A.M. until around 12:00 midnight, although they are run less frequently in the evening.

One of the best ways to explore the French countryside is by car. Rentals and less expensive leases are available. In general, driving and parking in the larger French cities are best avoided. Cars can be rented at airports from major rental companies. Budget rentals are available, often in the cities, but finding them and arranging to get and return the car may not be worth the savings. Travel agents and travel guides are good sources of information.

7. Letters, Telegrams, Faxes, and Email

Mail service through the post office is excellent. Stamps can be purchased at post offices and *tabacs*. Telegrams can be sent from a post office, and every major city has at least one location open 24 hours a day. Fax machines are widely available.

Email is the quickest and least expensive way to send messages in and from France, but you have to have access to the Internet. Most international hotels now provide access and some even have business centers with computers available. The best way to get Internet access anywhere in France is to ask.

8. Shopping

Shopping in France is an adventure. While prices may not be particularly low, the quality of what you buy is usually excellent. Besides insisting on quality, shopkeepers typically take great care with the appearance and display of the products they sell.

In France, one can find many items for sale in individual specialty shops. Thus, fish is sold in a *poissonnerie*, bread in a *boulangerie*, meat (pork, beef, lamb, poultry) at the *boucherie*, horsemeat at the *boucherie chevaline*, sausage and other prepared meats at the *charcuterie*, vegetables at the *marchand de legumes*, and so on.

FIRST STEPS

The *epicerie*, or grocery store, usually serves also as the *crémerie* where milk, cream, and dairy products are sold. Larger markets selling a combination of products are common in France and are called *supermarchés*. Mall-like *hypermarchés* with one or more anchor stores and many smaller specialty shops are becoming popular in France as they are elsewhere in the world.

Traditionally, French people do their food shopping on a daily basis, and in many families this tradition continues today. This makes it possible to have fresh bread, milk, meat, and vegetables every day. You will need to bag your selections, and most people take baskets or *filets* (string bags) to carry their purchases home.

Shops in France are often closed from around noon to 2:00 or 3:00 P.M. daily (except certain department stores), and some small neighborhood grocery stores may be closed from 1:00 until 4:00 P.M., and then stay open later into the evening. Shops are closed on Sundays and Monday mornings.

For other types of purchases, department stores afford variety as well as competitive prices. Some of the best-known chains are: *Au Printemps, Galéries Lafayette, Au Bon Marché, Trois Quartiers,* and *Samaritaine.* Sales are often held in January and during the last weeks of June and July.

9. Health and Medical Care

Water is safe to drink in most of France unless it is marked *nonpotable*. In fact, France is known for its spring waters, some of which are helpful for specific illnesses or medical conditions. Bottled water is available everywhere and is commonly used by everyone. Some varieties are carbonated. Pasteurized milk is available and safe; however, since not all milk is pasteurized, you should check to make sure when you order any, particularly in smaller farm towns.

The International Association for Medical Assistance to Travelers, Inc. (IAMAT) is a useful source of information for locating approved English-speaking doctors. Membership in the organization is free, and prices for doctor visits are set. France has 29 hospitals and clinics that are members of IAMAT. For information in the United States, write to IAMAT, 736 Center Street, Lewiston, NY 14092.

10. Security

In the larger cities in France, skilled pickpockets can quickly identify foreign visitors as easy targets. It is important to remember to carry your purse or bag firmly and to keep an eye on your belongings in airports and train stations. The Paris *métro* is a favorite haunt of pickpockets, who often work in pairs: one will "accidentally" knock against you while the other opens your bag or purse to remove your wallet. They do not even need to take the whole bag!

Be sure not to carry your passport, tickets, and all your cash or travelers' cheques with you when you go out into a large city. Put what you have to carry into different compartments in your purse or carrying bag. If you are staying in a hotel, leave what you don't need to carry in the manager's safe.

11. Tipping

In France, service charges are included in your hotel bill but are listed separately on your restaurant checks. To make sure they

FIRST STEPS

are included, check for *service compris*. If you are not certain, be sure to ask. If service is included, you are not obliged to leave any additional tip, but it is common to leave a little extra, particularly in more expensive restaurants.

In hotels, the service charge covers everyone except the baggage porter, who will expect a small tip, and the *concierge* (hotel porter), whose tip will vary depending on the length of your stay and the amount of special service you demand of him or her.

At cafés and bars, the tip is always included in the bill. Train porters get a fixed fee, which is indicated on a metal tag on their overalls. In theaters and movie houses, and at sports events, you are expected to tip the people who show you to your seat. If your are unsure about what to tip in any situation, check with a French friend about the appropriate amount. Information about tipping in taxis is given in section 6 on Transportation; it is not mandatory.

12. Electricity

There are no ll0-volt electrical outlets in France. All outlets are for 220-volt appliances. Outlets have holes for three round prongs. Before you leave the U.S., you can buy adapters to attach to your appliance plugs when traveling.

FIRST STEPS

13. Conversions

In Europe sizes and measures differ from those used in the United States. The following charts will help you make the necessary conversions if you are not already acquainted with the European system.

Measurements
Weights and Linear

Metric	U.S.
1 gram (g)	0.035 ounce
454 grams	1 pound
1 kilogram ("kilo")	2.2 pounds
1 centimeter (cm)	0.3937 inch
2.54 centimeters	1 inch
1 meter (m)	3.280 feet
1609.3 meters	1 mile

Liquid Measure

1 liter (l)	2.113 pints
1 liter	1.056 quarts
3.785 liter	1 gallon

Dry Measure

1 liter	0.908 quart
1 dekaliter (10 l)	1.135 pecks
1 hectoliter (100 l)	2.837 bushels

Kitchen Equivalents

Metric	U.S.
200 grams	1 cup sugar
150 g	1 cup flour
5 g	1 tsp.
12 g	1 tbsp.

FIRST STEPS

Kilometers and Miles

1 km	0.6 mile	25 km	15.5 mile
3	1.8	35	21.7
5	3.1	50	31.0
8	4.9	100	62.1
10	6.2	200	124.2
15	9.3	300	186.4
20	12.4	500	310.6

Thermometer Readings*

38°C	100.4°F	0°C	32°F
35°	95°	-5°	23°
30°	86°	-10°	14°
25°	77°	-15°	5°
20°	68°	-17.77°	0°
10°	50°	-25°	-13°
5°	41°	-30°	-22°

*European thermometers use the centigrade scale. To convert Fahrenheit to centigrade, subtract 32, then multiply by 5 and divide by 9. To convert centigrade to Fahrenheit, multiply by 9, divide by 5 and add 32. The chart above gives an approximate conversion. 21°F=69.8°F

If you don't have a calculator handy or the time for long-hand calculations, this very rough rule of thumb will give you the approximate Fahrenheit equivalent of centigrade temperatures: the centigrade temperature times two plus 30 equals the approximate Fahrenheit, or C° x 2 + 30 = F° (approx.).

Clothing Sizes

Skirts, Dresses, Coats:

Europe	U.S.
38	10
40	12
42	14
44	16
46	18
48	20

Blouses:

Europe	U.S.
38	30
40	32
42	34
44	36
46	38
48	40

Shirts:

Europe	U.S.
36	14
37	14½
38	15
39	15½
41	16
42	16½
43	17

Shoes:

Europe	U.S.
37	6
38	7
39	8
40	9
41	10
42	11
43	12

2. Customs and Values

Now that you have a handle on basic facts about where to find what you need and how to get it, you will want to begin looking more closely at how people live in France. Since French people are to be your new friends and family, it is important to understand their customs and values so you can fit into their world successfully. The topics in this chapter have been chosen to help you begin your study of French customs and values. Again, it will be up to you to learn the specifics about the people with whom you live and interact. The information we give you here is only a place for you to start. This is the beginning of your cultural exploration; it will be up to you to complete it.

The following topics are covered in this section:

1. Greetings and Leave-takings
2. Names and Titles
3. Forms of Address
4. Conversation Topics and Style
5. Invitations
6. Privacy
7. Personal Appearance
8. Time
9. Meals
10. Family
11. Daily Life
12. Leisure
13. Cafés
14. National Pride

CUSTOMS AND VALUES

1. Greetings and Leave-takings

Social encounters in France have very clear beginnings and ends. A hand shake and kisses on the cheeks *(la bise)* are the most common forms of greeting and taking leave. The handshake, used even among close friends, consists of a single shake with a slight pressure on the grip. Women should offer their hands to men, not vice versa. People usually shake hands whenever they meet one another, even if they have seen each other only a few hours before. They also shake hands when saying goodbye to one another.

Kissing on the cheeks is the appropriate way to greet close friends and family. Different families and friends have different customs concerning the number of kisses: some greet with two kisses, one on each cheek; others greet with three kisses, on alternating cheeks; still others greet with four kisses, also on alternating cheeks. As you become more familiar with people, you will become accustomed to the number of kisses they expect.

When meeting people for the first time, French people are usually reserved. Personal questions about someone's family or way of life are not considered polite, so keep your conversation general at first.

When you enter a store in France, it is customary to greet whomever you are dealing with, as well as others in the shop, before you state what you need. When you leave, say goodbye. Appropriate expressions are *Bonjour, messieurs* (Hello), or *Au revoir, messieurs* (Good bye). Of course, *Au revoir, mesdames* may be called for if you are addressing women only, or *messieurs-dames* if you are addressing both men and women.

2. Names and Titles

Titles are an important part of social interactions, as they help the French identify and maintain roles and distances in relationships.

The French use the titles *Monsieur* (Mr.), *Madame* (Mrs.), and *Mademoiselle* (Miss) frequently in their conversation. When one of these titles is used to refer to you by someone talking to you, it indicates courtesy and an interest in your being involved in the conversation. *Mademoiselle* is generally used for young women; otherwise, *Madame* is considered to be more polite.

First names are used once people get to know each other, but if you use them too early, you may be seen as "pushy" or "rude." You should wait and let your French acquaintances indicate when it is appropriate to begin using first names.

3. Forms of Address

In French there are two forms for addressing another person as "you": *tu* and *vous*. The use of the correct form is important because it is a sign of the relationship that exists between you and the person to whom you are talking. The French are sensitive to the distinction between *tu* and *vous*, and using them appropriately can help you get along with French people.

The use of *tu* signals a closer, friendlier, or informal relationship, whereas *vous* indicates a formal, more distant relationship. There are no simple formulas for the use of each form, but a useful rule of thumb is to use *tu* with family, friends, children, and fellow students, and to use *vous* with other people in other situations. To move from *vous* to *tu* in a relationship, take your cues from the French person, who may make this shift during a conversation with you, or may openly suggest using *tu*. You can also ask if you may use *tu (On peut se tutoyer?)*.

4. Conversation Topics and Styles

For the French, conversations are the glue that holds relationships together. To an observer, a French conversation might seem like an argument, with people constantly interrupting or talking at the same time, apparently attacking one another with animated gestures, loud voices, and even laughter. What makes this a conversation instead of an argument is that the French enjoy challenging one another's views and opinions, stating and explaining their views. They readily express disagreement and expect others to do the same. Criticism is also expected and even welcomed. The French appreciate logical arguments, eloquence, wit, and humor. *How* you say something is just as important as *what* you say. If you accept French views on conversation, you may find it easier to build relationships with the French through conversations with them.

The French are willing to talk about almost any topic, but there are topics that they may consider too personal or intimate for some conversations. Take your cues for appropriate topics from the other people in the conversation.

5. Invitations

You should arrive on time in France when you have been invited for a meal. For a party, some delay in arrival is acceptable, up to half an hour after the stated time.

When you arrive, you should wait for the host or hostess to invite you inside. Usually he or she will help you with your coat and show you where to go or where to sit. It is polite to bring a gift of flowers (other than roses or chrysanthemums) or candy. When refreshments are being served, it is polite to stand up to take what is being offered. When seated, you should sit with your legs together or crossed; do not put your feet up on chairs or low tables.

It is of course important to thank your host and/or hostess, and thank-you notes are frequently sent the day after more formal gatherings. One should also shake hands with everyone at the party before leaving.

CUSTOMS AND VALUES

6. Privacy

The French respect their privacy. They prefer not to discuss personal matters with people who are not close friends or family. You should telephone if you want to visit someone; "dropping in" without warning is not appropriate. Doors in offices are usually kept closed, and you should knock before you enter an office or a room in a home where the door is closed if you know that someone is inside.

7. Personal Appearance

Historically, one's clothing and personal appearance have been important for the French. One's choice of clothing is a sign of individual style, and the French are very conscious of how they and others look. Whether a peasant or a prince, a punk-rock star or an international business executive, the French take their appearance seriously and, to most Americans, seem chic and slightly formal.

8. Time

Time is designated according to two systems in France. In official schedules, the 24-hour clock is used, where 01:00 means 1:00 A.M. and the hours are counted up consecutively to 24:00 (midnight). 13:00 means 1:00 P.M. The 12-hour clock is also used, and this system may be used in conversation instead of the 24-hour one. Be sure to clarify which system is being used when you make an appointment. For example, if someone says 8 *heures* and you are not sure what system she or he is using, you can easily clarify by asking *du soir?* (In the evening?) or *du matin?* (In the morning?). It could be either if the speaker is using a 12-hour system; it could only be in the morning if she or he is using the 24-hour system.

CUSTOMS AND VALUES

Punctuality is valued in France, although the time one is expected to arrive varies with the event. For any official appointments, you will be expected to arrive on time. This is also true for meetings with friends if you are getting together at a specific location to do something or go somewhere else.. If you are meeting at a *café* to relax and enjoy yourselves, prompt arrival at the time specified is less expected. (See section 5 on Invitations.)

9. Meals

Meals in France are social events to be savored and enjoyed, and the French tend to spend longer at meals than you might expect. The only exception is breakfast. Traditionally, the main meal was eaten at noon during a two- to three-hour break. Customs are now changing in the larger cities, and many families have the main meal in the evening. Still, the traditional noon meal is important and may be served on the weekend even if not during the week.

In France, people keep both their hands visible on the table when they are seated for a meal. This is done by resting your forearms on the edge of the table when you are not actually eating. It is considered impolite to put your elbows on the table. When eating, the fork is held in the left hand and the knife is held in the right. The fork is held upside-down, and the knife remains in the right hand even when you are not using it to cut something. The left hand is used to manipulate the fork for eating so the knife can remain in the right hand at all times. Those who are used to using the right hand for eating with a fork may need some practice at eating in this manner. The end of the knife and fork should be balanced on the edge of the plate when they are not in use. When you are finished eating, they should then be laid across the plate.

It is also considered impolite to talk with food in your mouth, and to drink from your glass without having first wiped your mouth with a napkin.

Bread is served with all meals in France, and pieces should be broken off with the fingers rather than cut with a knife. Similarly, lettuce in salads, which is usually served in large pieces that cannot be easily fitted into the mouth, should be folded with the fork and knife and never cut.

CUSTOMS AND VALUES

10. Family

The French family is very close-knit, and family loyalties are important. Family members spend a lot of time together, and attendance at family gatherings—weddings, baptisms, and the like—is expected of everyone. The extended family can be quite large, and it is not uncommon to find grandparents living with their children and grandchildren. Young French people are in general very respectful of their adult relatives and often spend as much time with them as they do with peers, although this is beginning to change. Although the father of a French family plays a dominant role, it is the mother who usually runs the household. Family life is private, and when someone outside the family is invited home, it is usually an important sign of acceptance and friendship.

11. Daily Life

The average working day in France begins between 8:00 and 9:00 A.M. Traditionally, there is a two- to three-hour break at noon for lunch. In this case, the working day ends between 6:00 and 7:00 P.M., and dinner is served around 8 P.M. or later. Parents often take their children to school on their way to work. Non-working parents do the daily shopping once the rush-hour traffic has ended.

At noon everyone returns home for lunch. Parents will often collect the children at school so they can be home for the midday meal. Although lunch is traditionally the main meal of the day, this custom is changing in large cities where it is common to find the "continuous day" with only a 45-minute break for lunch. In this latter instance, the workday ends earlier. The traditional pattern is still observed by many small businesses and in smaller towns. In the afternoon, people return to work and children go back for an afternoon school session. Schools close for a half day on Wednesday but are open for classes on Saturday morning.

On weekends, people usually stay home and do work around the house or have large family gatherings with members of their extended family. Some families have country homes to which they travel on weekends.

CUSTOMS AND VALUES

12. Leisure

While the French enjoy watching certain team sports like soccer, rugby, basketball, and volleyball, they are more apt to participate in individual ones such as cycling, windsurfing, mountain climbing, skiing, hiking, jogging, and tennis.

The French enjoy reading newspapers, magazines, and books, and are usually well informed and up-to-date. There are dozens of different publications in France, targeted for many different audiences. Some sample categories are: sports, religion, politics, literature, fashion, women, *presse du coeur* (romance), and youth.

The family vacation is the high point of the year and is usually taken sometime during July or August. Often a mother who is not working will take the children to the country or seaside, and the father will join them for the five weeks he is legally allowed off from work. While away, the mother may take the children to the beach or river for swimming, or send them to a *colonie de vacances* (vacation resort) where such activities are supervised. Once the father joins the family, however, they act as a unit again and go most places together.

13. Cafés

Cafés are popular throughout France. In the morning, you can get delicious coffee and *croissants* at a café. Most also serve sandwiches and snacks in addition to beverages. There is no age limit for drinking in France, so anyone can go to a café (although children probably will not be served alcoholic beverages). It is important to develop a taste for relaxing in a café and talking with friends, since this is an important pastime in France.

CUSTOMS AND VALUES

14. National Pride

The French are very proud of their country and its national achievements. Their history, which dates from prehistoric times, fires this pride. This attitude has caused them to be somewhat insular in their viewpoints and sometimes a bit unadaptable when traveling abroad; however, national pride is a very important part of the French character and can be appreciated when accepted as part of their culture. The French are also particularly proud of their language. They attach great importance to speaking French correctly, and they tend to point out errors and supply correct forms in a very direct manner.

3. Country Facts

As you become more comfortable living in France, you will find that you will want to know more about the country; for example, how it is organized and governed. This section includes information about the following aspects:

1. History
2. Maps
3. Land and People
4. Government
5. Economy
6. Education
7. Religion
8. Art

1. History

The French are proud of their history and, as a result, France's past remains very much alive today. The earliest inhabitants of France were there a hundred thousand years ago, and some of their prehistoric settlements have been preserved in the *Vezere* valley, in *Font-deGaume,* and in *Lascaux*.

The first ethnic group to inhabit France were called Ligurians, and the French people today are of Ligurian origin. Their ancestry also contains Celtic blood, since the Celts (also called Gauls) conquered the Ligurians in the 5th century B.C.

In 58 B.C., the Roman conquest of the Gauls began. These wars, known as the Gallic Wars, lasted ten years, at the end of which Rome had taken over control of Gaul. The Romans ruled it for 500 years. Lyon is the city that was established by Rome to be the economic and political capital of the Province of Gaul.

COUNTRY FACTS

Sully-sur-Loire was built in the 1100's to guard a crossing of the Loire. It was the royal residence away from Paris of the Dauphin *(Crown Prince) when in 1429 Joan of Arc, a farmer's daughter turned warrior who had just raised the siege of Orléans for him, finally convinced him to go with her to Rheims to be crowned Charles VII. Later she herself stayed at Sully for a month just before she was captured and handed over to the English under King Henry IV to be tried and then burned at the stake as a witch. Joan, the Maid of Orléans, is now the patron saint of France.*

Gaul remained relatively peaceful until the beginning of the 5th century A.D., when barbarians from the north invaded. These Germanic tribes lived on friendly terms with the Gauls, once they had set up their own territories. The Franks were one of these tribes, and France was later named after them. The Franks eventually became rulers and, under the leadership of Charlemagne and the emperors who immediately preceded him, the empire was extended to the Baltic Coast, Russia, mid-Italy, and the Pyrenees.

Following Charlemagne's death, no one leader was strong enough to rule the country, and the empire became fragmented. Feudalism was born and continued through the Middle Ages. *Carcassonne* is a walled town built in this period.

In the 13th century, France emerged as a nation, one of the earliest countries to progress from feudalism to being a nation-state. Its monarchs were competent and its armies the most disciplined in Europe. Under the leadership of Louis XIV, from 1643 to 1715, France was the leading power in Europe. *Versailles,* originally a hunting lodge, was remodeled to its present grandeur by Louis XIV.

AVIGNON

Avignon, on the Rhône River, is one of several small French cities that still maintain some of their medieval architecture and walls. The bridge at Avignon, built in the 12th century as the first to cross the Rhône, is famous as the subject of a French nursery rhyme; nobody dances across the bridge today because it fell down, like London Bridge in the English rhyme. From 1309 to 1377 Western Christianity was split when a series of seven "French" popes rivaled the Italian popes in Rome, ruling from the still beautiful Palais des Papes *in Avignon.*

COUNTRY FACTS

Chambourd, the largest of the many great chateaux on the Loire, was started in 1519 by Francis I as a hunting lodge, a base from which to indulge his passion for hunting the plentiful deer, boar, and wolves of the forest of Chambourd. He summoned many of the finest architects and artists of the High Renaissance, many from Italy. Over fifteen years, about 1,800 craftsmen created this 440-room fantasy of spires, towers, chimneys, and over a hundred intricate staircases, including a central double helix invented by Leonardo da Vinci. Francis I made only a few short stays at Chambourd to enjoy the hunting.

During the 18th century, intellectual development reached its peak, but at the same time the privileges granted to the aristocracy gave rise to discontent among the peasants and the middle class. This finally resulted in the French Revolution (1789–1794), which established republican and egalitarian principles of government. After the Revolution, France returned to monarchical governments four times, under Napoleon, Louis XVIII, Louis-Philippe, and Napoleon III. After the Franco-Prussian War (1870–1871), the Third Republic was established, and it lasted until the defeat of France by Germany during World War II.

World War II brought great losses to France. After its defeat in 1940, France remained occupied by the Germans until it was liberated by the Allied Forces in 1944. Then, after a short period of provisional government, the Fourth Republic was established under the leadership of General Charles de Gaulle. His government was based on a parliamentary form controlled by a series of alliances among various factions. Because of this mixture of factions involved in governing the country, it was impossible to achieve agreement during various international crises confronting France. In particular, decisions had to be made about civil disturbances occurring in Indochina and later in Algeria, areas where France had colonies. It was, in fact, disputes over how to handle Algeria that led to the collapse of the Fourth Republic.

In 1958, de Gaulle rewrote the Constitution to strengthen the powers of the president in the hope that this would guarantee political stability for France. He, himself, was elected the first president of the Fifth Republic under this new Constitution. De Gaulle remained in power for another eleven years, until 1969. He was followed by Georges Pompidou, who took over the Gaullist Party. In 1974, when Pompidou died in office, his finance minister, Valery Giscard d'Estaing, won the presidency. He was not a Gaullist himself, but he appointed a Gaullist prime minister.

In 1981, François Mitterand defeated d'Estaing, and Socialist party candidates took the majority of the parliamentary seats. For the first time, France's government was Socialist. At first, Mitterand experienced high public ratings, but, as economic difficulties increased during the 1980's, the polls indicated a change in opinion; his popularity slipped. He was re-elected in 1988, but the political shift away from the left and toward right-wing candidates continued.

In April 1995, Jacques Chirac was elected president with a majority of conservative votes. Two years later, in April 1997, as his government was facing economic and social problems, Chirac dissolved the Assembly. After elections, a majority of the seats went to the opposition from the left. Lionel Jospin, a Socialist, became prime minister. This situation is referred to as *cohabitation*.

Notre Dame de Paris *cathedral on the* Ile de la Cité, *the historic center of Paris. This important religious site and cultural treasure is also a major tourist attraction.*

In recent years, there has been much discussion about decentralization. The tradition in France has been to centralize the affairs of state through Paris and the offices of the government there. Over the years there have been attempts to diversify the places of decision-making, to provide wider input into the decision-making process. The events of *mai 1968*, the widespread protests initiated by students, were a motivation to this end. The idea and practice of centralization, however, remain an ingrained cultural tradition among many French people.

COUNTRY FACTS

Napoléon Bonaparte, a Corsican soldier, ended the social chaos of the Revolution and then crowned himself Emperor of France. His disciplined armies conquered much of Europe and parts of the Middle East and North Africa before he was finally defeated at Waterloo. He profoundly changed the government, law, military, education, taste, the fine arts, and popular culture in France and the rest of Europe. This "first modern dictatorship" is generally judged to have done more good than harm to the people of France.

Related to this tradition of centralization is a strong sense of French nationalism. Most of the French take pride in the "glory" of French culture and in France's political independence. However, it is said that the French never agree about anything. For example, during World War II, the French government in Vichy collaborated with the Germans, but there was a strong French Resistance (guerrilla movement), and General de Gaulle, at the head of his Free French army, was a very independent member of the Allied Command. After the war, de Gaulle led France to join NATO, but he resisted the influence and leadership of the United States, as have all French presidents since then. In 1966, de Gaulle withdrew France from NATO's integrated military command. France then joined West Germany in establishing *détente* (a peaceful understanding) with the U.S.S.R.

General Charles de Gaulle, after the fall of France to Nazi Germany in World War II, organized those military elements that had escaped capture into an army that he allied with the British, Russians, and the U.S. After the war, he twice served as president of France and in 1958 peacefully ended the Fourth Republic and founded the present, more stable Fifth Republic under a new constitution. Perhaps because of his arrogant self-confidence, he succeeded in most of what he tried to do and left a strong and very independent nation as his legacy.

The Eiffel Tower at night. This emblem of 19th-century French industrial inventiveness and power now also suggests the power of French commercial interests.

At the same time that this French nationalism was flourishing, France was also leading the movement to a united Europe. Frenchmen Robert Shuman and Jean Monnet, along with Belgian Paul Henri Spaak, are considered to be the founders of the historic movement which has led to the present European Community (EC) and the 1991 Maastricht Treaty on European Union. The French still disagree with one another on how much military, political, and economic independence France should maintain within the European Community. They voted to ratify the Maastricht Treaty by only 51% on September 20, 1992. This same debate is going on in all the other nations of Europe, but it is particularly intense and politically important in France.

France has also assumed a major role in promoting *La Francophonie*, the promotion of the French language and its many cultural manifestations in countries around the world.

COUNTRY FACTS

A Brief Outline of French History

c. 4000 B.C.	Neolithic hunters begin to farm in France.
c. 600 B.C.	Phoenician and Greek traders colonize the Mediterranean coast. Marseille is founded by Greeks.
c. 500 B.C.	Indigenous Ligurians are overrun by Celtic tribes, the Gauls.
58 B.C.	Roman legions under Julius Caesar begin the conquest and unification of Gaul, adding all of it to the Roman Republic by 51 B.C.
50 B.C.-A.D. 406	Gaul prospers as a province of the Roman Empire.
406	German Vandals invade Gaul, followed by 80 years of chaos as Gaul and the Empire are overrun by Visigoths, Franks, and Burgundians. Attila the Hun briefly conquers Gaul and then is defeated in 451 A.D. at Chalôn.
486	Clovis, king of the Franks, unites France and founds the Merovingian dynasty, the first "French" kingdom.
732	Charles Martel defeats the Muslim Saracens. His son Pepin founds the Carolingian Dynasty in 751. His son Charlemagne enlarges the kingdom and is crowned the first Holy Roman Emeror in 800 by the Pope at Aachen. After Charlemagne's death in 843, his empire is divided in two kingdoms, which are now France and Germany.
911	Vikings settle in Normandy. France is torn by warlords like the Dukes of Normandy, Burgundy, and Aquitaine.
987-1337	The Capetian Dynasty begins with a strong king, Hugh Capet, who unifies France ruling from his capital of Paris. In 1066 the French under Norman Duke William the Bastard conquer England. Sainted King Louis IX leads the last Crusade but dies in Tunis in 1270.
1337-1589	The Valois Dynasty begins with the Hundred Years War with England 1337-1453 and the Black Death 1348-1350. Joan of Arc inspires French victories but dies burned as a witch by the English in 1431. In 1453 the English are finally defeated. Françoise I 1515-1547 revives royal power and glory; he is a great builder and patron of art.
1589-1789	The Bourbon Dynasty begins with Protestant Henry IV, who becomes Catholic and with the Edict of Nantes allowing some freedom of religion ends the Wars of Religion. In the long reign (1643-1715) of Louis XIV, known

COUNTRY FACTS

	as the Sun King, French royal power reaches its zenith and with it classical French culture flourishes.
1789-1804	The French Revolution begins with the fall of the Bastille fortress in Paris, July 14, 1789. A reign of terror under Robespierre and the Directory sends many leaders of the *Ancien Regime* to die on the guillotine, including the King, Louis XVI, in 1793. General Napoléon Bonaparte takes over the government as First Consul in 1799.
1804-1814	The Empire begins as Napoléon crowns himself Emperor. He conquers most of Europe but destroys his army trying to conquer Russia in the winter. He abdicates and is exiled to the island of Elba.
1814-1848	The Bourbon Restoration begins as Louis XVIII is put on the throne by the Congress of Vienna. Then Napoléon escapes for a Hundred Days, regains some control of France, but is defeated at Waterloo and exiled on the remote South Atlantic island of St. Helena, where he is secretly poisoned.
1848-1914	The Bourbons are replaced by Napoléon's nephew, Louis-Napoléon, elected to head the Second Republic. He then seizes power as Napoléon III, heading a Second Empire in 1852. France loses the Franco-Prussian War in 1871, and the Third Republic begins. This is a period of rapid industrial, trade, and colonial expansion. France dominates the world of art.
1914-1946	France fights two "World Wars" with Germany. WWI is fought with the aid of allies including Britain and the United States mostly, on French soil. After ten years of flourishing art and trade followed by ten years of worldwide financial depression, Germany attacks again under the Nazis. In 1940 in WWII the Germans conquer France but are again defeated in 1944 by the Allies, including the Free French under Charles de Gaulle.
1946-present	The Fourth Republic set up under de Gaulle is characterized by revolts in colonial Indochina and North Africa and great governmental instability. De Gaulle retakes control in 1958, bringing in a new constitution and greatly increasing presidential power. The more stable Fifth Republic has seen power shift from the Gaullists to the Socialists under François Mitterand in 1981 and then in 1995 to a rightist coalition under Paris mayor Jacques Chirac.

COUNTRY FACTS

2. Maps

Traditional Regions of France

COUNTRY FACTS

Cities of France

3. Land and People

Regions: France is divided into 21 administrative regions containing 95 *departments*. In addition, there are 5 overseas *departments*: Guadeloupe, Martinique, French Guiana, Reunion, and Saint-Pierre and Miquelon; plus 5 overseas territories: Vanuatu (formerly New Caledonia), French Polynesia, Wallis and Futuna Islands, and French Southern and Antarctic Territories; and one special-status territory: Mayotte.

Population: The population of France is about 56 million. It grows at a rate of about .5% per year, one of the lowest rates in the world. Seventy-seven percent of the people live in cities. The population density is 252 people per square mile.

People: The French people are a mixture of various European and Mediterranean ethnic groups. Historically, the Celtic, Latin, Germanic, and Basque peoples have been predominant in different regions of the country. Over the centuries, these peoples have blended so that today only a few distinctions are made on the basis of the original groups. However, the French are often very proud of their local and regional heritage.

Immigrants: Traditionally, France has had a high level of immigration. The two largest minority groups are South Europeans and North Africans. Among other groups are Slavic and Indochinese. In recent years, there have been attempts to limit immigration and benefits granted to immigrants. A small but vocal political party, *Le Front National,* has been in the forefront of this movement.

Language: The French language comes historically from the vernacular Latin that was spoken by the Romans in Gaul. Its grammar derives basically from Latin, although it contains many Celtic and German words in its vocabulary. (See page 53.)

Geography: France is the largest West European country. Two-thirds of the country is flat plains and gently rolling hills; one-third is mountainous. It covers 555,670 square kilometers (212,668 square miles) and is bordered by Belgium, Luxembourg, Germany, Switzerland, and Italy to the northeast and east, the

Mediterranean Sea and Spain to the south, the Atlantic Ocean to the west and northwest, and the English Channel *(La Manche)* to the north. Its major rivers are *La Seine, La Loire,* and *La Garonne* in the west and north, *La Rhône* in the southeast, and *Le Rhin* in the northeast. Its major mountain ranges are the Alps and Aura in the east and the Pyrenees on the border with Spain. In the south center of the country is a mountainous plateau called the *Massif Central.*

Cities: Paris is the cultural and political capital of France. Other major cities include Marseilles, the large port city on the Mediterranean founded by the Phoenicians in 600 B.C.; Bordeaux, center of the *bordelais* wine region; Lyon, a major commercial and industrial center; Strasbourg, an important port on the Rhine and seat of the Council of Europe; Nice, a popular resort city on the Riviera; and Toulouse, *la ville rose,* famous for its many buildings constructed of red brick.

CHENONCEAUX

Famous Tourist Attractions: There are many attractions in France, but this list will suggest just a few. First of all, there are the vestiges of the Roman Empire that remain standing (or partly standing) to this day—the ancient aqueduct in *Nîmes,* the arenas in *Nîmes* and *Arles,* the theater and the arch in *Orange,* and other remaining structures throughout the south of France. The medieval era has left traces in the many castles, fortifications, monasteries, and cathedrals throughout France—impressive structures such as the cathedrals of *Notre Dame* in Paris, of *Chartres* in Chartres, of *Mont Saint Michel* in Normandy. There is also the string of chateaux along the valley of the river *Loire.* In many places in France, one can also see the legacies of the many wars that have been waged on French soil over the centuries – the statues in the plazas and parks, the monuments in town squares, the many cemeteries from World Wars I and II, and the blockhouses on the beaches of Normandy. Visitors to the various regions of France also seek out the many museums with treasures of French art and civilization. (See page 49.)

Climate: France's climate is temperate, with the northern half characterized by more extremes of temperature and rainfall than the southern half. The wettest regions are the *Massif Central*, the Aura, the Alps, the Pyrenees, and the northwest and west coasts around the Cherbourg peninsula, Brittany, and the Landes. The driest regions are the Paris basin and the Mediterranean coast.

4. Government

France is a republic governed by a president and a parliament composed of two houses, the Senate and the National Assembly. The National Assembly is the principal legislative body, and its members are elected directly by the people for a five-year term. All seats are voted on in each election. Members of the Senate are chosen by an electoral college for a nine-year term. One-third of the Senate is renewed every three years. The Senate's legislative powers are limited by the fact that the National Assembly makes the final decision in the event of disagreement between the two houses.

The Constitution of the Fifth Republic gives the president of the Republic certain powers over the Parliament: the president chooses the prime minister, presides over the cabinet, commands the armed forces, and concludes treaties. He or she may also submit questions to a national referendum and can dissolve the National Assembly. In certain emergency situations, the president may assume full powers. He or she is therefore the dominant element in the constitutional system. However, the National Assembly can force the dissolution of the government and call new elections if an absolute majority of the Assembly votes a censure motion.

The major political parties in France are the Socialist, Gaullist, and Communist parties, and a number of smaller parties referred to collectively as the Center parties: Independents, Moderates, and Republicans.

In the past, decisions have usually been made by the central government, which has also appointed the head of each department. In 1982, however, the national government passed laws to decentralize authority by giving many administrative and fiscal powers to locally elected officials.

Although the French government is politically independent, its policies are increasingly determined and limited by the European Community. Under the 1991 Maastricht Treaty, the 12 member nations must coordinate and then integrate their economies and many of their social policies. They are to have a common currency and common defense and foreign policies. There are to be no traditional borders to affect the free movement of people or capital. In all European nations, the power of the European Council of Ministers, Commissions of the European Communities, European Parliament, and European Court of Justice is increasing relative to the power of the national governments.

5. Economy

France's economy is growing and modernizing. France is, in fact, one of the world's leaders in industry and agriculture. It has large agricultural resources and a highly skilled labor force. The industrial enterprises are diversified and modern.

In 1981, following the election of Socialist François Mitterand as president and a Socialist majority to Parliament, a major change in economic orientation was initiated. Many large manufacturing firms were nationalized, as were most of the commercial banks. Initially, these changes stimulated growth. The policies were designed to redistribute income and increase government spending awhile controlling unemployment. However, since the policies differed considerably from those of France's partners in international trade, a resulting increase in import demand was not met by an equal increase in exports. By 1983, a growing trade deficit and inflation rate were straining the currency, and the *franc* finally had to be devalued. The present government policies are designed to stabilize the economy, with reductions in the budget deficit, cuts in spending, increases in taxes, and tighter monetary and credit policies.

The most important areas of industrial production in France are steel and related products, aluminum, chemicals, and mechanical and electrical goods. The country has been successful in developing dynamic telecommunications, aerospace, and weapons sectors.

France is a leading agricultural producer in Western Europe for a number of reasons: a temperate climate, large amounts of fertile land, use of modern technology in farming, and government subsidies. Major exports are dairy products, meat, wine, barley, and wheat. Although most land is devoted to pasture and grain, much of the country's best land is used to produce wine grapes.

In the 1990's, the economic policies of the French government are no longer fully independent. The French have their own economic and political agendas, but they must make their economic plans according to the General Agreement on Tariffs and Trade (GATT) and coordinate them with the trade, industrial, agricultural, and fiscal policies of the Common Market of the European Community (EC).

6. Education

France is proud of its government-controlled educational system, which is particularly excellent at primary and secondary levels. It is highly competitive and free of charge from kindergarten through the graduate level.

Children begin school at the end of their second year, when they enter an *école maternelle* (nursery school) for three years of non-compulsory pre-primary education. The emphasis at this time is on physical and sensory exercises, language development, and observation skills. Compulsory education begins with primary school at the end of the child's fifth year and continues for five years. At this point, the "secondary stage" of education officially begins.

LE PUY

Secondary education is divided into two cycles. Early in the first cycle, children are divided into those who will probably continue secondary school until the end of the second cycle and those who will not. The former group will continue until they are 18 years of age; the latter will receive a "terminal" degree and leave secondary school at the age of 16. For those completing the second cycle, there is an examination called the *baccalaureat* that must be passed in order to go on to higher education.

In higher education, there are two types of schools. One is the university, to which passing the *baccalaureat* guarantees admission. The other is what is known as a *grande école*. Competition for entrance into a *grande école is* strong and often requires two years of preparation. These schools specialize in a variety of subjects: literary, scientific, administrative. Some of the more prestigious ones are: *Ecole Normale Superieure, Ecole Polytechnique,* and *Ecole Nationale d'Administration (ENA)*. These schools are all located in Paris.

For many years the French educational system, with the help of the government, has tried to protect and enhance French culture. Noteworthy have been the attempts of *L'Académie Française* to maintain the purity of the French language by discouraging the use of foreign words and phrases. (See Chapter 4, "The French Language.") The government also has promoted the development and exposure of the French broadcasting, music, and film industries through subsidies and regulation requiring, for example, that a certain percentage of broadcasting in France be of French origin. Most French people are proud of the high quality of French culture, although music from other countries, and films and television programs from the United States, are very popular in France, as in the rest of the world. Non–French speakers sometimes feel intimidated because the French are exacting in their expectation of "proper" French usage; if your French is "rusty," they will reply to you in English. It may make you more comfortable to realize that French parents and teachers are quite strict in their expectations that their own young people speak their language correctly, and the French are actually relatively tolerant of non-native speakers.

7. Religion

The majority of French people are baptized Roman Catholics, but only one in five is active in the church. After childhood, the majority may have contact with their church only at their marriage ceremony, the baptism of their children, and the funerals of family and friends. The most active Catholic areas of France are Brittany in the west, Alsace in the east, and the southern area of the *Massif Central.*

There are also six Protestant denominations; they make up the *Federation Protestante de France.* Of these, three are Reformed Churches, two are Lutheran, and one is Baptist. The highest proportion of Protestants is in the *Bas-Rhin department* in Alsace and in the *Card department* in the south.

Islam and Judaism are the principal minority religions. The Jewish community is one of the most active in Western Europe, with most members residing in Paris, Marseilles, and Alsace.

8. Art

If there is one defining characteristic of French culture, perhaps it is the confidence that most French people share that their culture is of great importance to world civilization and has been as long as France has been France. The French, of course, appreciate the cultures of the other European nations like Spain and Germany, and from time to time they have enjoyed a passionate interest in the arts of more exotic places in Asia, Africa, and the Americas. But they have great pride in the arts of France, and they know that for hundreds of years Paris has been the capital to which artists of all kinds have come for inspiration and recognition. There are French people who are not interested in the arts, but even they know how central those arts are to what it means to be French.

What are those arts? Music, painting, sculpture, literature, theater, dance, and film are touched on below, but only lightly. This is an arbitrary choice, and even about these arts there is too much basic information to summarize meaningfully. There are other arts at which the French excel, notably architecture, landscaping and gardening; clothing design and the design of machines of all kinds, furniture, tableware, and pottery; the production and selection of wine; professional and domestic cooking. And perhaps the two most basic French arts, the art of living, of seeking quality in small, transient pleasures, and the social arts, the gentle art of hospitality and graciousness and the more aggressive art of conversation.

Music: Since the Middle Ages, there have always been important composers and musicians in France. Today there is all kinds of music everywhere, from Paris to the smaller towns in all parts of the country. The best way to find live performances is to ask. The music scene today is naturally as varied as the population; it may be professional or homespun, classical, international, jazz, pop, or ancient or modern folk music, in churches, schools, theaters, and cafés. France's greatest contemporary composer-conductor, Pierre Boulez, helped make Paris one of the world's liveliest centers for contemporary music. He took over responsibility for a new experimental music center in the Pompidou/Beaubourg arts complex in 1977, and it is here that most activities occur.

In concert halls like the Salle Pleyel in Paris, you will hear great performers from all over the world. Although France has contributed its great talents like flutist Jean Pierre Rampal, today's top musicians and orchestras are all international. During the first part of the 20th century, two popular music stars, Edith Piaf and Maurice Chevalier, became so well loved that they were accepted as symbols of French culture, of the French spirit, not only in France but all around the world. They were international stars, but they were intensely French. Since their deaths, although there have been many great popular French singers, none has gained the international recognition of Piaf or Chevalier. Nevertheless, there are many good French cabaret and jazz artists and pop and rock groups in France today.

The controversial glass pyramid of I. M. Pei in the courtyard of the Louvre Palace in Paris serves as a visitors' center and museum shop.

Painting: The modern art of painting was first developed in Italy and Flanders, not in France; during the past three hundred years, however, France (particularly Paris) has often been at the creative forefront as styles of painting have developed, and famous painters from all over the world have spent part of their careers living and working there. Many well-known works can be found in French museums. When you are in Paris you should be sure to spend some time at the *Louvre,* the world's largest royal palace, where one of the world's largest art collections is housed.

COUNTRY FACTS

At the Louvre Museum in Paris, two of the most famous pieces of art in the world, the Venus de Milo (left) and Leonardo da Vinci's Mona Lisa (right), known by the French as "La Joconde"

Other worthwhile art museums in Paris include:

Musée d'Orsay, a museum with a wonderful collection of Impressionist and Post-Impressionist 19th and 20th century paintings.

Jeu de Paume and *Orangerie*, two small museums with exhibits of challenging avant garde art and paintings by Impressionists Monet and Renoir respectively.

For most of the 20th century, the French Impressionists and Post-Impressionists have drawn larger crowds to exhibitions, sold more posters, postcards, and calendars, and brought higher auction prices than any other group of artists. Manet, Monet, Renoir, Degas, and Cézanne, Van Gogh, Gauguin, Toulouse-Lautrec, and Matisse are as popular in Tokyo and Chicago as they are in Paris. Their works may be found in many musems throughout France.

Like most of Auguste Renoir's work, "End of the Luncheon" captures the light, lively color, sensuality, and "joie de vivre" that seem essentially and delightfully French to all the world.

Musée National d'art Moderne, which contains contemporary painting and sculpture.

51

Centre National d'art et de Culture Georges Pompidou, which has permanent exhibits of works by 20th century artists and organizes special exhibits twice a year.

Sculpture: One of the best known nineteenth-century sculptors was Auguste Rodin, a master of the realist tradition. Some of his works can be seen at the *Musée Rodin* in Paris. In the 19th and 20th century museums mentioned previously, there are more Rodins and works by other French sculptors like Antoine Bordelle, Aristide Maillot, and Charles Despiau, as well as work by non-French sculptors who worked in France.

Literature: France is justly proud of its literary tradition, which includes many of the greatest poets, playwrights, novelists, and philosophers in history. Some of the most renowned French authors are Rabelais, Mme. de Stael, Montaigne, Descartes, Pascal, Molière, Racine, Voltaire, Rousseau, Stendhal, Victor Hugo, George Sand, Balzac, Baudelaire, Flaubert, Guy de Maupassant, André Gide, Colette, Proust, Rimbaud, Rostand, Albert Camus, Jean-Paul Sartre, and Simone de Beauvoir.

Theater and Dance: In Paris the Comédie Française and the Opéra perform the classics of French drama, ballet, and opera. But there is theater and dance everywhere in France, performances for everyone's tastes. Seek out the small, out-of-the-way theaters and the cabarets, both the classics of Paris nightlife like the Crazy Horse, the Moulin Rouge, and the Folies Bergére and the less touristy small cabarets and jazz clubs to be found in towns all over France.

Film: The French enjoy watching films from many countries, but they also have a thriving cinema industry of their own. The French place special value on film directors, believing that they are the key artists in cinema. Going to see the latest film directed by Jean-Luc Godard, or to a festival of films by François Truffaut, is just as common as going to see films starring famous actors and actresses such as Gerard Depardieu and Catherine Deneuve. The best of the world's new commercial films are shown at the Cannes Film Festival each May. Rare and classic French films are shown in Paris at the Pompidou Center and the Musée du Cinéma.

4. The French Language

More than 90 million people speak French as their mother tongue. It is an official language of Canada, Switzerland, Belgium, Luxembourg, Haiti, and a number of countries in West and Central Africa, and also of the United Nations. In fact, French is so widely spoken that it is considered an international language. Despite some variation in pronunciation, vocabulary, and grammar, French-speakers from different regions can usually understand one another.

French belongs to the Romance family of languages—along with Spanish, Italian, Portuguese, and several others. These languages all have their origin in ancient Latin. French began with the conquest of Gaul (France) by the Romans around 50 B.C., when the Gauls gradually began to use the informal Latin of the Roman soldiers. This language changed with the invasion of the Franks about 400 A.D. and again with the later invasion of the Danish Vikings (Normans) around 800 A.D. French first appeared in written form during the 9th century. As it developed, French had two major dialects, North and South. Because of the political influence of Paris, the dialect spoken there in the North became the accepted form throughout France. In the 17th century, the structure of French began to be standardized through the efforts of writers and scholars. It was during this period that the French Academy *(L'Académie Française)* was founded by Cardinal Richelieu; one of its tasks was to develop a standard dictionary of the French language. Modern French has been somewhat influenced by other languages, including English (at least since 1066), Modern Italian and Spanish, and Greek. Like all living languages, particularly international ones, French continues to grow and evolve.

The use and the richness of the French language have expanded over the last four hundred years as the French colonial empire expanded into North, West, and Central Africa, into Southeast Asia, to the South Pacific, to North and South America, and to the Caribbean. In France, *L'Académie Française* has tried with some success to maintain the integrity of their language, but inevitably both the French language and culture have evolved as the French traded with peoples all around the world. Today the era of colonialism is past, but many former French colonies, now independent countries, have retained French—*their* French—as an official language.

THE FRENCH LANGUAGE

1. Some Basic Grammar

Following is a brief outline of the essential features of French.

Articles

Nouns in French are either masculine or feminine. Articles agree in gender and number with the noun.

1. Definite article (the): *le, la, les*

	singular			**plural**	
masculine	*le garçon*	the boy	*les*	*garçons*	the boys
feminine	*la maison*	the house	*les*	*maisons*	the houses

2. Indefinite article (a/an): *un, une, des*

	masculine				
masculine	*voyage*	a trip	*des*	*voyages*	(some) trips
feminine	*une lettre*	a letter	*des*	*lettres*	(some) letters

Nouns

1. Nouns are generally made plural by adding **s**

	singular		**plural**	
after consonants	*garçon*	boy	*garçons*	**boys**
after vowels	*lettre*	letter	*lettres*	letters

There are exceptions,.

	cadeau	gift	*cadeaux*	gifts
	journal	newspaper	*journaux*	newpapers

2. To show possession, use the preposition **de** (of).

la porte de la maison	the door of the house
la valise de Jean	Jean's briefcase
la chemise du* garçon	the boy's shirt
les maisons des** hommes	the **men's** houses
les chaussures des** enfants	the children's shoes

*du is the contraction of *de* & *le*.
**des is the contraction of *de* & *les*.

THE FRENCH LANGUAGE

Adjectives

1. Adjectives agree with the nouns they describe in gender and number.

	singular		plural
masculine	*petit*	small, little	*petits*
feminine	*petite*		*petites*
masculine	*long*	long	*longs*
feminine	*longue*		*longues*

Most adjectives form their plurals, as do most nouns, by adding *s*.

2. As a rule, the adjective follows the noun.
    une lettre formelle
    but not always
    un petit garçon

3. Possessive adjectives.

	singular	plural
my	*mon/ma*	*mes*
your	*ton/ta*	*tes*
his/her/its	*son/sa*	*ses*
our	*notre*	*nos*
your	*votre*	*vos*
their	*leur*	*leurs*

Possessive adjectives agree with the thing possessed, not with the possessor. For example:

	singular	
	singular	
masculine	*son livre*	his or her book
feminine	*sa chambre*	his or her room
	plural	
masculine	*ses livres*	his or her books
feminine	*ses chambres*	his or her rooms

THE FRENCH LANGUAGE

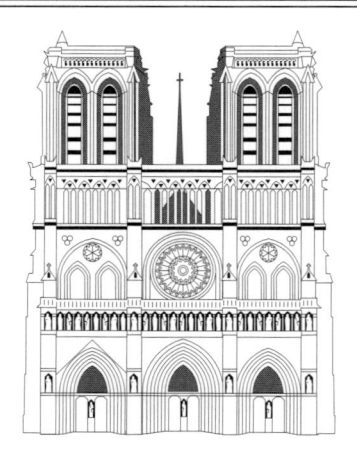

4. Comparative and superlative are formed by adding *plus* (more) or *moins* (less) and *la/le plus* (the most) and *la/le moins* (the least).

belle	beautiful
plus belle	more beautiful
la plus belle	the most beautiful
moins belle	less beautiful
la moins belle	the least beautiful

Adverbs

Adverbs generally are formed by adding *-ment* to the feminine form of the adjective.

masculine	**feminine**		**adverb**	
lent	*lente*	slow	*lentement*	slowly
doux	*douce*	soft	*doucement*	**softly**
heureux	*heureuse*	happy	*heureusement*	happily

There are exceptions.

bon	*bonne*	good	*bien*	well

Adjectives are sometimes used as adverbs, e.g., *fort* can mean strong or strongly, *vite* can mean quick or quickly.

56

THE FRENCH LANGUAGE

Pronouns

1. Possessive pronouns.

	singular	plural
mine	le mien/la mienne	les miens/les miennes
yours	le tien/la tienne	les tiens/les tiennes
his/hers/its	le sien/la sienne	les siens/les siennes
ours	le/la nôtre	les nôtres
yours	le/la vôtre	les vôtres
theirs	le/la leur	les leurs

Possessive pronouns agree with the thing possessed, not with the possessor. For example,

singular
masculine *Le livre est le mien.*
    The book is mine.
feminine *La chambre est la mienne.*
    The room is mine.

plural
masculine *Les livres sont les miens.*
    The books are mine.
feminine *Les chambres sont les miennes.*
    The rooms are mine.

2. Demonstrative pronouns.

	masculine	feminine
this	celui-ci	celle-ci
these	ceux-ci	celles-ci
that	celui-là	celle-là
those	ceux-là	celles-là

Ceux-là sont ses livres.   Those are his/her books.
Elle aime celui-ci.   She likes this one.

THE FRENCH LANGUAGE

3. Personal Pronouns

	subject	direct object	indirect object
I	*je*	*me*	*me*
you (fam.)	*tu*	*te*	*te*
you (pol.)	*vous*	*vous*	*vous*
he	*il*	*le*	*lui*
she	*elle*	*la*	*lui*
it	*il/elle*	*le/la*	*lui*
we	*nous*	*nous*	*nous*
you	*vous*	*vous*	*vous*
they	*ils/elles*	*les*	*leur*

Elle vous la donne.   She gives it to you.

Verbs

1. There are two important **auxiliary verbs:**

    être (to be)
    je suis (I am)
    tu es (you are)
    vous êtes (you are)
    il/elle est (s/he is)
    nous sommes (we are)
    vous êtes (you are)
    ils/elles sont (they are)

    avoir (to have)
    j'ai (I have)
    tu as (you have)
    vous avez (you have)
    il/elle a (s/he has)
    nous avons (we have)
    vous avez (you have)
    ils/elles ont (they have)

THE FRENCH LANGUAGE

2. And three main categories of **regular verbs:**

Infinitive:	ends in -**er** **parler** to speak	ends in -**ir** **finir** to finish	ends in -**re** **vendre** to sell
je	parle	finis	vends
tu	parles	finis	vends
il/elle	parle	finit	vend
nous	parlons	finissons	vendons
vous	parlez	finissez	vendez
ils/elles	parlent	finissent	vendent

3. **Irregular verbs:** As in many languages, exceptions have to be learned separately. The following are four common irregular verbs:

	pouvoir to be able to, can	*aller* to go	*voir* to see	*connaître* to know [a person]
je	peux	vais	vois	connais
tu	peux	vas	vois	connais
il/elle	peut	va	voit	connait
nous	pouvons	allons	voyons	connaissons
vous	pouvez	allez	voyez	connaissez
ils/elles	peuvent	vont	voient	connaissent

Negatives

Form the negative by placing ***ne*** before the verb (or auxiliary) and ***pas*** after it.

C'est difficile.   It's difficult.
Ce n'est pas difficile.   It's not difficult.

Questions

Form questions by changing the intonation of your voice, raising the last word, or by using the question marker *Est-ce que*.

Vous parlez français.	You speak French.
Vous parlez français?	Do you speak French?
Est-ce que vous parlez français?	Do you speak French?
Il est au restaurant.	He's at the restaurant.
Il est au restaurant?	Is he at the restaurant?
Est-ce qu'il est au restaurant?	Is he at the restaurant?
Vous vendez des fleurs.	You sell flowers.
Vous vendez des fleurs?	Do you sell flowers?
Est-ce que vous vendez des fleurs?	Do you sell flowers?

Question Words

qui?	who?
quoi?	what?
pourquoi?	why?
quand?	when?
où?	where?
d'où?	where from?
jusqu'où?	where to?
comment?	how?
combien?	how much?/how many?

Pourquoi est-ce que vous vendez des fleurs?
   Why do you sell flowers?
Où est-ce que vous vendez des fleurs?
   Where do you sell flowers?
Quand est-ce que vous vendez des fleurs?
   When do you sell flowers?

THE FRENCH LANGUAGE

Can. . .?

Can I have . . . ?/ Can you give me . . . ?	*Pouvez-vous me donner . . . ?*
Can we have . . . ?	*Pouvez-vous nous donner . . . ?*
Can you show me . . . ?	*Pouvez-vous me montrer . . . ?*
Can you tell me . . . ?	*Pouvez-vous me dire . . . ?*
Can you help me, please?	*Pouvez-vous m'aider, s'il vous plaît?*

Wanting

I'd like . . .	*Je voudrais . . .*
We'd like . . .	*Nous voudrions . . .*
Please give me . . .	*S'il vous plaît, donnez-moi . . .*
Please bring me . . .	*S'il vous plaît, apportez-moi . . .*
I'm hungry.	*J'ai faim.*
I'm thirsty.	*J'ai soif.*
I'm tired.	*Je suis fatigué(e).*
I'm lost.	*Je suis perdu(e).*
It's important.	*C'est important.*
It's urgent!	*C'est urgent!*
Hurry up!	*Dépêchez-vous!*

It is . . . / There is . . .

It is . . .	C'est . . .
Is it . . . ?	Est-ce que . . . ?
It isn't . . .	Ce n'est pas . . .
There is . . . / There are . . .	Il y a . . .
Is there . . . / Are there . . . ?	Il y a . . . ?
There is no . . .	Il n'y a pas . . .
There are no . . .	Il n'y a pas . . .

Prepositions, conjunctions, and adverbs

behind	derrière	inside	dedans
to	à	outside	dehors
for	pour	down	en bas
until	jusqu'à	up	en haut
toward	*vers*	above	au-dessous
since	depuis	along	le long de
through	par/à travers	between	entre
at	à	on	sur
in	dans/dedans	under	sous
during	pendant	none	aucun
with	avec	and	et
without	sans	or	ou
before	avant	also	aussi
after	après	perhaps	peut-être
soon	bientôt	not	ne ---pas
already	déjà	nothing	rien
then	puis	nobody	personne
again	encore	now	maintenant
there	là	immediately	toute de suite
here	ici	gladly	avec plaisir

THE FRENCH LANGUAGE

Some common words

cheap / expensive	*moins cher / cher*
good / bad	*bon / mauvais*
better / worse	*meilleur / pire*
true / false	*vrai / faux*
light / heavy	*léger / lourd*
easy / difficult	*facile / difficile*
full / empty	*plein / vide*
vacant / occupied	*libre / occupé*
open / shut	*ouvert / fermé*
old / young	*agé / jeune*
old / new	*ancien / neuf*
big / small	*grand / petit*
quick / slow	*vite / lent*
beautiful / ugly	*beau / laid*
warm / cold	*chaud / froid*
never / always	*jamais / toujours*
early / late	*tôt / tard*
near / far	*près / loin*
left / right	*gauche / droite*
yes / no	*oui / non*

THE FRENCH LANGUAGE

Quantities

a little / a lot	un peu / beaucoup
much / many	beaucoup / beaucoup
more than / less than	plus que / moins que
enough / too	assez / trop
some	de la / du / des
any	de la / du / des

Numbers

Cardinal

1	un, une		19	dix-neuf
2	deux		20	vingt
3	trois		21	vingt et un
4	quatre		22	vingt-deux
5	cinq		30	trente
6	six		40	quarante
7	sept		50	cinquante
8	huit		60	soixante
9	neuf		70	soixante-dix
10	dix		71	soixante-onze
11	onze		80	quatre-vingt
12	douze		90	quatre-vingt-dix
13	treize		91	quatre-vingt-onze
14	quatorze		100	cent
15	quinze		101	cent et un
16	seize		120	cent-deux
17	dix-sept		1000	mille
18	dix-huit			

THE FRENCH LANGUAGE

Ordinal

1st	*premier, première, 1ᵉʳ*	18th	*dix-huitième*
2nd	*deuxième, 2ᵉ*	19th	*dix-neuvième*
3rd	*troixième*	20th	*vingtième*
4th	*quatrième*	21st	*vinième*
5th	*cinquième*	30th	*trentième*
6th	*sixième*	40th	*quarantième*
7th	*septième*	50th	*cinquantième*
8th	*huitième*	60th	*soixantième*
9th	*neuvième*	70th	*soixante-dixième*
10th	*dixième*	71st	*soixante-onzième*
11th	*onzième*	80th	*quatre-vingtième*
12th	*douzième*	90th	*quatre-vingt-dixième*
13th	*treizième*	91st	*quantre-vingt-onzième*
14th	*quatorzième*	100th	*centième*
15th	*quinzième*	101st	*cent et uneième*
16th	*seizième*	1000th	*millième*
17th	*dix-septième*		

THE FRENCH LANGUAGE

2. Useful French Phrases

Greetings

Good morning.	*Bonjour.*
Good afternoon.	*Bonjour.*
Good evening.	*Bon soir.*
Good night.	*Bonne nuit.*

Approaching Someone

Excuse me.	*Excusez-moi*
• Sir	*Monsieur*
• Ma'am	*Madame*
• Miss	*Mademoiselle*

Do you speak English?	*Parlez-vous anglais?*
Do you understand English?	*Est-ce que vous comprenez l'anglais?*
Yes/No.	*Oui/Non.*
I'm sorry.	*Je suis désolé.*
I don't speak French.	*Je ne parle pas français.*
I don't understand.	*Je ne comprends pas.*
I understand a little.	*Je comprends un peu.*
I speak very little French.	*Je parle très peu de français.*
Please speak slowly.	*Parlez lentement, s'il vous plaît.*
Please repeat.	*Répétez, s'il vous plaît.*
Thank you.	*Merci.*

THE FRENCH LANGUAGE

Asking for Help

Excuse me. — *Excusez-moi.*
May I ask a question? — *Une question, s'il vous plaît?*
Could you please help me? — *Pourriez-vous m'aider?*

Identifying Yourself

I'm a tourist. — *Je suis touriste.*
We're tourists. — *Nous sommes touristes.*
I'm not from here. — *Je ne suis pas d'ici.*
I'm from the United States. — *Je suis des Etats-Unis.*
I'm from New York. — *Je suis de New York.*
  • Philadelphia — *Philadelphie*
  • Chicago — *Chicago*
  • California — *Californie*
I'm American. — *Je suis américain(e).*
We're Americans. — *Nous sommes américains(es).*

Asking for Information

What time is it, please? — *Quelle heure est-il, s'il vous plaît?*

Where is the men's / ladies' room? — *Où sont les toilettes?*

Where is a subway station? — *Où est le métro?*
Where is the police station? — *Où est le commisariat?*
Where is the post office? — *Où est la poste?*
Where is a mail box? — *Où est la boîte à lettres?*
Where is a good restaurant? — *Où est un bon restaurant?*

How much does this cost? — *C'est combien?*
How do you say "Please" in French? — *Comment dit-on "please" en français?*

THE FRENCH LANGUAGE

Politeness/Courtesy

Please.	*S'il vous plaît.*
Thank you.	*Merci.*
You're welcome.	*De rien.*
Sorry (excuse me.).	*Pardon.*
Excuse me.	*Excusez-moi.*
Good appetite.	*Bon appetit.*
It doesn't matter.	*Ça ne fait rien.*

Leave-taking

See you soon.	*A bientôt.*
So long.	*Salut.*
See you later.	*A toute à l'heure.*
See you later.	*A plus tard.*
See you tomorrow.	*A demain.*
Good-bye/Bye.	*Au revoir.*

Some Books about France

Berkeley Budget Guides: France - On the Loose, On the Cheap, Off the Beaten Path, by University of California at Berkeley students. New York: Fodor's Travel Publications/Random House, revised periodically.

Berlitz Pocket Guides: France. Oxford/Berlitz Publications Ltd., 1996. (Also available, guides to other places in France.)

Blue Guide: France, by Ian Robertson. London/New York: A & C Black/W.W. Norton, 1997.

Culture Capsules: USA–France, World Culture Series, by Dr. J. Dale Miller and Maurice Loiseau. Salt Lake City, Utah: Culture Contrasts Company, updated periodically.

Cultural Misunderstandings: The French-American Experience, by Raymonde Carroll. Chicago: University of Chicago Press, 1988.

Cycling in France by Carole Saint-Laurent. Montreal: Ulysses Travel Publications, 1997.

Cycling France: The Best Bike Tours in All of Gaul, by Jerry H. Simpson, Jr. San Francisco: Bicycle Books/Motorbooks International, 1992.

Fodor's France by Fodor's Modern Guides. New York: David McKay Company, revised annually. (Also available, guides to other places in France.)

France (Library of Nations Series) by Time-Life. New York: Time-Life, Inc., 1985.

France: Its People and Culture, Focus on Europe Series, edited by Lynn M. Hilton, Ph.D. Skokie, Illinois: National Texbook Company, 1982.

SOME BOOKS ABOUT FRANCE

France: The Hungry Traveler Menu Translator and Food Guide, by Sarah Belk King. Kansas City: Andrews McMeel Publishing, 1997.

France: Michelin Tourist Guide. London: Michelin Tyre Public Ltd. Company, updated annually. (Also available, guides to other places in France.)

France Today: The Journal of French Travel and Culture, a monthly magazine. San Francisco: France Today.

France: Traveller's Literary Companion, containing over 120 extracts from novels, poems, travel writing, and short stories, by John Edmondson. Chicago: Contemporary Publishing Company, 1997.

French or Foe? Getting the Most Out of Visiting, Living and Working in France, by Polly Pratt. , Yarmouth, Maine: Cultural Crossings, Ltd., distributed by Intercultural Press, Inc., 1995.

Insight Guides: France, edited by Anne Roston, et al. Boston: Houghton Mifflin Company, 1994. (Also available, guides to *Brittany, Burgundy, Côte d'Azur, The Loire Valley, Paris,* and *Provence.*)

Mind Your Manners: Managing Business Cultures in Europe (New Edition) John Mole. Yarmouth, Maine: Nicholas Brealey Publishing, distributed by Intercultural Press, Inc., 1995.

La Belle France: The Sophisticated Guide to France, a monthly newsletter. Charlottesville, Virginia: Travel Guide, Inc.

Let's Go: France, edited by Robert C. Lagueux, et al. New York: St. Martin's, revised annually. (Other guides available.)

Life in a French Town, by D. L. Ellis. London: Harrap, 1979.

Living in Paris, by José Alvarez, photography by Christian Sarramon and Nicolas Bruant. Paris/New York: Flammarion, 1996.

The French-Speaking World: An Anthology of Cross-Cultural Perspectives, by Louise Fiber Luce. Lindenwood, lllinois: National Texbook Company, 1991.

SOME BOOKS ABOUT FRANCE

Paris: For Free (or Extremely Cheap): Hundreds of Free and Inexpensive Things to Do in Paris, by Mark Beffart. Memphis, Tennessee: Mustang Publishing, 1997.

Paris Guide: Be a Traveler – Not a Tourist, by Robert F. Howe and Diane Huntley. Cold Spring Harbor, New York: Open Road Publishing, 1998 (email Jopenroad@aol.com).

The Riches of France: A Shopping and Touring Guide to the French Provinces, by Maribeth Clemente. New York: St. Martin's Griffith, 1997.

The Rouge Guide: France, by Kate Baillie and Tim Salmon. London/New York: Rouge Guides, Ltd., 1997.

Savoir Vivre en Francais: Culture et Communication, by Howard Lee Nostrand, Frances B. Nostrand, and Claudette Imberton-Hunt. New York: John Wiley and Sons, 1988.

The South of France: No Poodles, No Shades, No Attitudes, by Danna Facaros and Michael Pauls. London: Cadogan Books, plc, 1997. (Also available in series: **Provence** by Facaros and **The Loire** by Phillippe Barbour.

Time Out Guide: Paris, by Natasha Edwards. Paris/London: Time Out/Paris: Penguin Books, revised periodically.

Understanding Cultural Differences: Germans, French and Americans by Edward T. Hall and Mildred Reed Hall. Yarmouth, Maine: Intercultural Press, Inc., 1990.

Also Available from Pro Lingua Associates

Living in Italy
Living in Germany
Living in Greece
Living in Japan
Living in Mexico
Living in Spain
Living in the United States

and for the teacher

Cultural Awareness Teaching Techniques
by Jan Gaston

Taking Students Abroad
A Complete Guide for Teachers
by Maggie Brown Cassidy

Index Card Games for French
edited by Raymond C. Clark

Families
10 Card Games for Language Learners
by Fuchs, Critchley, and Pyle

Beyond Experience
The Experiential Approach to Cross-Cultural Education
revised edition edited by Ted Gochenour

Lexicarry
An Illustrated Vocabulary Builder for Second Languages
with a French Word List
by Patrick R. Moran

Notes

Take this little book along with you on your adventure. As you explore French culture, observations and suggestions we have made will probably take on new and greater significance. But, if you use these last pages or take along a traveler's notebook, in the future your personal notes will be the most important observations of all. You think you will always remember the name of that little café in Carcassonne where you ate on the terrace by the old city gate. What did they call that locally famous stew? What was that wonderful wine? And what was the name of your special French friend? Take one last piece of advice, take notes.

Notes